ABOUT THE AUTHOR

clare e. potter is a poet and radio presenter who studied an MA in
Afro-Caribbean literature in Mississippi and taught in New Orleans. She
facilitates creative projects with community groups and is motivated by
the belief that poetry can be a force for personal and social change.
Recently, Wales Arts International funded her to take part in a poetry
therapy conference (USA). Other awards include a Literature Wales
writing bursary, a Society of Authors grant, and funding from the Arts
Council for a poetry/jazz collaboration to respond to the trauma of
Hurricane Katrina. clare has had poetry residencies with the Landmark
Trust and Moravian Academy and performed at the Smithsonian Folklife
Festival in Washington DC. She was a Hay Festival Writer at Work and
has created poetry installations in public spaces with local people. clare
directed a BBC documentary (The Wall and the Mirror) about her village
barber, thereafter a group formed to save the local miners' institute. clare
has translated for the National Poet of Wales, Ifor ap Glyn, and has
presented several BBC radio poetry programs; as a result of being Poet
of the Month for Radio Cymru, she began a Welsh poetry pamphlet, *Nôl
Iaith*, which will be published with Cyhoeddiadau'r Stamp. She is
currently mentoring other artists, facilitating writing for wellbeing
workshops and preparing *The Dragon's Pen*, a forthcoming BBC radio
Wales programme. *Healing the Pack* is her second poetry collection.

PRAISE FOR *HEALING THE PACK*

'In *Healing the Pack*, clare e. potter claims her place as one of our most important Welsh poets writing today. Rooted in Welsh landscape and culture, these poems give primacy to the viewpoint of mother, which is not a sentimental role but a vital one. The connection to and nurturing of children in this collection is profound, but it also means the narrator must look back on her younger self, cataloguing difficulties for girls growing up. In writing about violence against women and girls, potter registers the wider harm and legacy of trauma for the whole family. In poignant experiences mediated via the natural world and family, the narrator heals herself but also works towards healing the entire family and community – the pack of the collection's title. This is the poet as magician, as healer, and as conduit for the more-than-human: the wisdom of nature beyond human knowledge. *Healing the Pack* is a moving and beautiful collection, which I will be returning to for comfort and inspiration again and again.' **Zoë Brigley**

'In *Healing the Pack*, clare e. potter offers us poems of great personality and impact. She writes from the right place always, straight out of the heart, and it is rare to find poems so capable of capturing personalities that we feel we are right there in the room with the people in these poems. The writing is full of tenderness for parents and children, rich in explorations of the past, and travels from the terraces and mountains of South Wales, to the southern states of the USA. I love the worldview and insight of these poems, the way they've formed a language which is capable of expressing the special connectedness of people in the communities of South Wales. Just as, in one poem, a boy bends a piece of wire 'to get into the gubbins of something,' so these poems show us what's really inside ourselves – all the beauty and all the care for each other that's sitting there.' **Jonathan Edwards**

'clare e. potter's poetry is perfect pitch,: ironic, daring, she writes with emotional intensity but also with sensual vibrancy. These poems are intimate explorations, discovering truths in fine particulars and in unexpected ways. We are all the richer for reading her and throughout her work she 'risks delight'. She's a poet who goes all out to articulate an energy which ultimately startles the mind of the reader.' **Menna Elfyn**

'I have waited eagerly for another collection from clare e. potter. I felt Immediately pulled into her moving new book where I found myself leaning close to its inhabitants to hear powerful, ringing testimony. *Healing the Pack* has made me consider how a family holds itself together, how it carries its past into the future; how this is achieved through language and love.' **Rebecca Goss**

clare e. potter
Healing The Pack

For Suzanne

with love and gratitude

Clare

VERVE
POETRY PRESS
BIRMINGHAM

PUBLISHED BY VERVE POETRY PRESS
https://vervepoetrypress.com
mail@vervepoetrypress.com

FIRST PUBLISHED MAY 2024

Printed and bound in the UK
by ImprintDigital, Exeter

ISBN: 978-1-913917-54-8

Cover artwork: 'Axis Mundi' by Lucy Campbell
www.lupiart.com

FOR MAM AND DAD

CONTENTS

KEEP CALM, MAM, AND WRITE POETRY

Notes and Acknowledgements

Healing
The Pack

This is my church, this is where I heal my hurts
—God is a D.J., Faithless

Mam, let's not go on the path we know,
let's go on the path we don't know

Quick, take this stick
dip it in the brook
so I can write that down.

Bird Prayer I: Chick

When she was carrying me, my teen mother,
pennies in her pocket, walked over the Showfield where
autumn had dragged summer's yolk into September;

she crossed fields and hills, making her way
to the river to silence a gaping beak.

Above the dingle, the peregrine dive-bombed—
tear-shaped sky-stone, unsheathed talons
snatched the fat ground-bird to feed

her young. My mother wiped
the blood from her mouth.

Whose Footsteps?

My mother, generation stiletto
fishnets, Panache, Sun-In, Youth Dew.
Don't be fooled though by lipstick stuck
fast with Lipcote, for when my father got home,
there was dinner on the table, news on.

My mother, generation stiletto
worked in the factory, night-shifts on tip-toes.
My mother, self-raiser, left alone
by her own mother— out cleaning
for pennies, dancing till late at the local.

My mother left in the dead quiet house to read,
her only company the clock ticking; by the self-stoked
fire, my mother washed her school socks
and knickers, mixed her own watercolours.
She painted her way out, child bride, child

mother, taught me to draw, to sing;
in unison
we were two girls growing together.

My mother
generation stiletto
bought me boots for stomping, so
I could go
where I aimed to. She wears flats now, places
toes down first as she walks, out of stiletto custom,

I tell her, *Heel-toe Mam! Keep your back straight.*
You're tall enough, Mam, without them.

'She Wouldn't Be Able to Come to You So Often If She Were Alive'
Kim Hyesoon

It's when I'm washing, usually, the dishes,
it's when I'm lost in a heat of suds
and I'm looking out the window, not staring
mind you, not fixed on anything but not really
seeing, it's then, it's then I feel her. I feel her
hand on my shoulder, and now I think of it:
the first time, when the kids were babies
when I was delirious and brushing bottles
and teats, decontaminating and weeping into the sink
standing in my piss, and there, her hand on my shoulder—

that first touch was a light touch
not on account of her being dead of course,
but on account of her not wanting to shock
me, on account of her bringing me back
into myself, knowing, *Look,*
the touch said, *look at the fly in the window,*
the white rabbit on the grass.

Wish You Were Here

Under the bed, in the lidless biscuit tin, I found old postcards
to Tessa 1957 to '62:

Hope you're OK now,
        love Lil.

Hope the weather improves soon.

Hope you're getting along all right.

No question marks or tales of donkey rides
or puppet shows. Pearl writes,

Hope you are well and in health, God bless you.

And Tessa's love, the miner gone to pieces, his concertina
card from the convalescent home by the sea,
Settling in, Tess. Letter to follow.

What did that letter want
to say, and if it was written
was it cherished or chucked in the fire

and what did those neighbours know,
those holidaymakers, keen to fill
the tiny space of separation with

Eating plenty.

See you Saturday.

See you Sunday.

See you soon?

Measuring the Distance

'The only landscape I see in dreams is the Black Mountain village in which I was born.' - Raymond Williams

(1880)
You are Sarah of Annie with the 18-inch waist
who once threw a stale bread at the vicar,
raven-haired Sarah with the malachite eyes
who does not yet know how histories of hangings
and beatings line up with their collective nudge
to be heard in the DNA of you—

                not Sarah of Welsh spoken
and Eisteddfod winning uncles, or political picnic speakers,
or of dry stone wallers, or the county's best sheepdog breeder,

but Sarah of   Sarah of   Sarah of

                with no idea why your neck hurts
and your temper burns and why you always break into song at night.

(1950)

In the dayroom by the window, a town away, a time away,

The prettiest meadow I ever saw was on an old coal tip,
she keeps repeating

the meadow I saw,   the pretty of it,   the old coal I saw,
how pretty I was,   the old cold sore tip,   the coal
all over the meadow   spoiling pretty.   In her dreams

there are no oxeyes, yarrow, campion, no grasses
sending patterns of shivers at her feet. In her dreams
she hears her father speak over the spitting liver, she fears
the belt coming off and her back still braces for its slap.

(2020)

And there you are, *my* father: kind,
different to me, content
with your *milltir sgwâr*, Dad, content
to travel deep, not wide.
No need to dream your landscape:
in daylight you move along its curves
wandering the old burial path, each step
brings you closer to your mother.

By the kissing gate, the gasp
as the red kite revisits the sky.

Through your walking and pausing, the past
confronts the present, and you have measured
each devoted step, with a true touch.

milltir sgwâr – square mile

Bedside Photo

After Hannah Lowe, 'If You Believe: On Salmon Lane'

If I'd met her (the one in the frame Dad made
when he was a boy)
I'd have understood why the house
went so grey after she died.
If I'd have been there, in Weston before
the pier burned down,
I'd be burning like him, little boy not
in the photograph,
off to the side, kicking dried dog shit
probably,
waiting for his father to tell her *Hold still*
by the flowers she didn't know the names of, dropping
the camera case, her not laughing. I tell you, I'd know why
she was clutching her scarf, the one she kept in the back
of her drawer,
I'd notice what her boy notices: the mole
on her calf, how she drapes
her cardi on her shoulders,
how small she looks, smile frail as moth wings.
If I could,
I'd people the place, bring in her *tada* who adored her
and the mother who died birthing her, and aunty so-and-so
who wet-nursed her in the old train carriage, I'd take
the name of the dead man
on the bench behind her and
revive him, let him share this rare, good day. And if I could,
I'd be begging for candyfloss,
to go on a carousel, to get off
a carousel with her and my father, the boy
beaming and dizzy,

the three of us without yesterday's sherry.
And there we'd be
on the Ferris wheel above all those clouds,
she'd be free
to put an arm around him and me and she'd not have left
him in school, motherless, with a file and wood, shaving
the layers,
trying for all his young life to make the frame
that would hold her still.

tada - grandfather

. . .

That's how my father tells it as he stands
in the road where she'd lived, his mother
she in the picture from the old town book
only 17, at the jubilee street party, leaning
to the left a little. Pretty as a rose bud all
about bloom, not yet
thinned out. Promise of cake and pie and
a stout maybe,
promise of clearing plates
back in a house
stuffed with love, happy the queen
or was it the king had come to the throne,
united before the war, before all those wars
that squatted on another street.

Code

We were a family of wordmakeruppers,
formed them in our garden's soil, Mam's balls of wool.
We were a tribe. A young trio of tongues
finding the words to bind us, make us
laugh, keep us knitted, planted, set us
growing and being grown together,
learning the shapes of individual mouths
then uttering or pulling one from the other, the morphemes,
the gutturals, the hums to sleep in *hwiangerddi*,
the happy-while-doing-a-job harmonies, the gesticulations,
the *Quick! Run for your life* sounds, and the dog,
at last, the dog, and with him
a new demotic: field spit and claw clack on kitchen floor,
oh, the way my father keened over him as he rubbed his jaw
and gently bit him on his snout in love—the words the dog
said back in pleasure,
the words the dog said
brought us together
all a bubble of mumbles and heartspeak
that only we could decipher.

hwiangerddi – lullabies

By Heart

After school I'm up the field learning vocab
for tomorrow's French test, the dog's zig-zagging
a scent, snouting out clouds of Yorkshire fog,
spikes of meadow foxtail. I read the grasses
parting for his seeking. When I close my slim book
try to recall *oeuvre* and *ouvre*, the hush and gather
of syllables brushes my legs
causes me to open my eyes, follow the shiver
of all the words that I've yet to discover.

Orientation

Though you liked to lean on your gate, watch
the people you knew,
you dreamed of London
and an Irish love. You'd save pennies for bus fare, tell me
double-decker stories on our way 'back home' to Peacehaven
pointing out all your years on both sides of the valley.

For months I've been mapping you in my dreams,
trying to pin you back in place now you're ash and giggle
on Mynydd Bedwellte. I'm trying to go where I can't be,
back to when we meandered the old railway line
with stick and colander for blackberries.

In sending me over the allotment for eggs, down the mill
where Islwyn had made poems, to Aunty Hilda's for 5p cards,
in sending me on errands beyond our lattice of streets,
in handing me betting shop pens and butcher paper, you were
        telling me

to map myself
to go with words that would also travel—
you were pointing out
longitude and sometimes latitude, teaching me,
when I've needed it most,
to read along these lines
and between them,
to find my way back to you.

Between Us

Separating our gardens, the breeze-block
wall patterned with a hollowed-out
flower. Before it threw me, I straddled
that rough horse, half on home-ground,
and squashed red velvet mites like

I had been bloodied in battle. Soon enough
I fell for it - the other side, because
there was a swing and paddling pool.
Surely, I ignored the terrible shed
with its stare of a window, the vice
on his work-table, and jaw-open door? No
amount of swinging over a lattice of roses,
carefully tended could let me unsee what I saw . . .

False Witness

I'm glad I told the lie
bare-faced, hot-faced lie
that stopped that neighbour in his tracks;
glad my seven-year-old tongue knew a thing
or two—rolling a cola cube, attempting a whistle,
working loose a wobbly tooth—
could snake its way around a word, even then:
dismantle a man.

Stop
I'd said
I can hear my mother calling
and you can hear her too!

Taking it Out

When my grandmother
When my grandmother chopped wood
When my grandmother chopped
wood split clean, the axe gleamed

When my grandmother chopped
not just for the wood but for the sound
for the chopping sound
I was safe

When my grandmother chopped
swung   heaved   halved

When my grandmother chopped wood
neighbours went indoors

When my grandmother chopped wood
even the axe understood.

You're gonna have to ride that beast—ride it out
and leave it in a field to graze.

Mam

Another Case for Murder

After Vernon Scannell

Sometimes I wish I'd been the girl who took spray paint
to the school wall, a compass to the desk. Wish I'd necked
bottles of Malibu by the river, caught cold sores from snogging,
allowed a boy to finger me behind the pool hall. But I

was *good*, orchestrated blushes when I heard swears,
honed shock when my friend had a baby at 14.
I put
my head down, kept my eye-line
on Scannell and Orwell,
wanted to kill Billy's brother
for killing Kes, and
my friend's father who docked
the tails off puppies, but

I sang in the choir—
even though I was told to mime
the high notes—
I beat the boys in tests, fearlessly
mixed chemicals—
until the explosion in the lab
that sent my blood to the ceiling—
I kept my head
down, my voice in check.
I got a boyfriend and
a Saturday job,
got myself in the paper for a debate
on vivisection
and ate cake with the mayor. I never
dyed my hair, pierced my lip or beat anyone up.

I could not unpin the grenade, could not let
my voice out.
Instead, I laid landmines:

                    watched you step.

Still

Stay close to the line, dolly peg the sheets we squelched in the bath, hoist up the pole so they blow like ship sails, turn our vessel to face the sun—our floating island with goosegog bush and horseradish leaves, big enough for umbrellas. Stay on the garden path as I feed slugs to our ferret and you talk about the only year the tree had plums. Stay there at the stump of the spruce which grew bigger than the house after twenty Christmases being taken in replanted, takeninreplanted. Stay frozen like the milk out of the bottle, hatchet at your shoulder poised between up and down, your nylon slippers scorch-marked from firespit. Stay as the sheets thwack and Rocky's jaw shhmacks and the aspen leaves shiver, steady the deck, tie a rope round me, keep me on board, don't go indoors to stoke the fire, peel potatoes, or do the pools; let's stay where the fruit is underfoot and never ever eat it.

Organic Matter

After Jorge Luis Borges, 'The Golem'

My father hated the pot I made in school
thought it looked too earthy with its swollen
ridges and rims and opening,
he'd shriek and joke and we'd laugh
how he couldn't stand to be in the same
room, as if it pulsed and had come to life.
He wanted to know why I couldn't
make a vase or trinket dish instead,

but I'd found this woman, womb neck and cervix,
her wide-open mouth
in the space between tree limbs
(though I hadn't known
at the time what was being shaped).

She began as coils thick as intestine
that I wound and moulded, squashed and rubbed—
my fingers slipping between what was inside
and what was out. Before firing,
I etched my name
at the base
so when I put my ear to the pot
her echo told all the secrets I could not.

Swyn-gân / Summoning

Pwll-y-Wrach the witches' cauldron
soup of iaith   words held and spoken

rhythm pulled by moon and tongue
hear its pitch from swell and belch
wrack and kelp of vowels sung

look now to this murmuring trickster
pre-linguistic meaning-maker

pull and pwll   push through bwlch
pull and pwll   push . . .

here the baptised words are brining
consonants reverberating
the tide's a swirl of incantation
sacred knowing being written
under chin of rock   the sea's graffiti

yr iaith gaeth ar y traeth
on shale of shore   the healing lip

wrach – witch; *iaith* – language; *pwll* – pool; *bwlch* – gap; *iaith gaeth ar y traeth* – formal/captive language on the beach (this nods to cynghanedd, the Welsh strict poetic form)

Bird Prayer II: Golden Eagle

Barranca del Cobre, after two hours
on dirt roads, my silent guide
lies on the bed of his pick-up, hat over his face,
asleep in seconds. Over the lip
of the steep ravine, I

scootch on my backpack, a hundred foot
wall of loose rock, petrified I am death-descending—
vultures sky-lurk tourists here. Sun and fear-
flushed, cuts gravelled, I reach them: paradise pools.

Beyond the boulders, sliding naked into my own
hot waters, on my back, a surrender
to the tapioca of bullfrog spawn, fingers
let go in a mass of beating hearts,
a thousand budding eyes until holy cries fill
the canyon and the golden eagle
riding the thermals I set to rising—
my joy as echoes, blessing.

This Current / Period

June 2020

the posy of blood in bed this morning
gave me the same shock as in form two
B Block toilets, my knickers a confession,
a scroll of sacred instructions.

I'd forgotten month cycles
that my body and the waves
were still talking with the moon.

The beauty in this flowered clot
was the reminder that though some things
are uncertain, my body is not.

You'll be Fine After the Funeral's Over, After the Last Fist of Earth

Burying things is not always bad
down there the winds of the wild
will leave the corpse to rot, will not
release a heavy soul from its trial
free it from the rigid bed.

That day, where I had my day
to speak all the dead ones back,
those banshees dragged his guilt
by his severed sac. After the hymns

sighed on being sung, I left the mourners
still deliberating. The sky though had made her decision,
the snow, all the snow was ash falling,
                    bone powder of his lies
and their last-burning.

Redress

The wall, I –
        I took a sledge hammer to –
the shed,   I –
            kicked down –
yanked the swing chain
            from the –
            threw the seat through
the greenhouse door
            smashed glass
            shattered—
        the bird trapped inside
the sky opened for its wings, tornado—

       I   tore   at   his   roses
I bled,   let
myself bleed there onto that neat grass

I gashed my knees on
the flagstones I'd chalked on
            hop
                scotched over the thrown stone

I found his vice
       I fed
       my fingers to its clamp
tightened my grip, I
on myself   –

     The dust
I blew from my –
clothes, shook my hair
         loose.

        I tore that fucking
        garden to debris –

I did not look back
to see the damage
I un
damaged
        – walked away
        I did;
        shined the apple on my sleeve.

Mam, you know when we are walking?
Only the mountain understands
what our feet are saying

On a Day When I've Been Struggling

We go out in storm Francis looking for berries before
they get blown off the bushes, for one last pie
or some for the freezer in case of another virus spike.
We're pushed across the bridleway, the wind a shepherd on our backs
so we are all red cheek, wild hair—strands like witches' fingers.

We put our pot under the blueblack fruit, lush and wobbling
on the stem. My girl is all lip, she is becoming the berry from within,
eating more than the fruit—
she is pip and thorn, leaf. Her tongue mulches root sense.

Between wind gusts, she bellows the question,
searching up at the hazel,
wild-haired like us,

> *But how do the nests stay still, Mam?*
> *How do the nests stay still?*
> *And why don't the birds fall out?*

If I Could Write a Poem the Way My Boy Turned the Corner

Didn't hold my breath,
suck down the gut shout of terror
that he'd scrape his knees to bone
and knock his teeth out, worse,
get his head run over by that car
mounting the pavement;

no momentary mind funeral,
I watched how he
        bone-
        skin-
        metal-
        concrete-
                trusted the bend

allowed himself with speed to leave air

graceful   fluent   at one with the wheels

at one with the ground's deep pulse   and how he

                                pushed

and glided
            and paused
                    and pushed
                        and glided

then
tail-whipped
his scooter
like he honed motion,

                  how he

                                        left my

Poams

When you were seven, I said I was giving up;
you broke from your colouring to ask, *What?*
Give up what, Mam? Maybe your child's ear
needed assurance I did not mean *you*
(I hadn't realised I'd said it aloud). *Poems,*
writing, trying to juggle all that, that's all.

You laid your blue down, deliberate,
shifted the tone in your voice so you became
my mother that time, potato in palm,
peeler pointing at me, sorting those tears out.

Well, you can't give up. You been doin them poams
since you was little, and look now, you got me
doin them too; and I'm brilliant!
Your words were a hoof to my doubt.

You let the dust of the kick settle,
then picked up your pencil
and finished the sky,
some spilled from the page onto the table—
the wide sky, which you later filled
with birds and other winged creatures.

Disappearing Act

Just now, my love dipped his head around the study door,
Oh, I thought we'd lost you, he said.

                            It's true, I've absented
myself from the arguments about maths and which kid
gets to use the laptop first, and the kitchen bomb blast
and the family meeting we have every morning. I have
skulked – like any creature with a wound does –
to the safety of my battered chair.

                         My love is thoughtful
he's left me here, thinks I'm reeling in a poem,
but his words are on my hook, gasping
and flicking their dreadful truth,

                              though he doesn't know it at all.

His Second Poem

composed when he was two
cwtched in a mass of bluebells
one foot turned in slightly,

Flower's happy cause flower crying

I clapped my hands, thought of apples
and trees and chips and old blocks
that he had wrapped his words around
a moment, or not the moment—
the beyond of it and I had been waiting
hands cupped for months to receive

his work, since his
Boy got a bee in the ear
had taught the doctor something
about the inside creature
which had tried eating his thoughts.

cwtched – cuddled

Seeing (Better than Looking)

She's three-and-a-half and though she does play dollies
what she really likes is foreheads together so we are eye-height
no blinking

> it reminds me of mirror-staring when I was little,
> trying to get in myself
> *Well who are you, you in the glass?*

When we have done our staring,
she slumps down
done with me

I ask what she did this morning in nursery,

> *I eatened a magpie*

and I seen **sk** *y*

'How the Light Gets In'

an exhibition on psychiatric genetics. She's no choice
but to take her sleeping boy who doesn't even wake
when she lifts him from the car. He's a hot lump
of dreams; she knows the time is sooning
where he'll be too heavy, too limbish
to carry, so she enters the art space
with her baby sling tight, palms his chubby face
to the pillow of her chest, their damp rise and fall.

She sits, displaces their lovely weight.
There are headphones to the film
which she listens into and hears women now speak
with air and space about the lack of those
and the post-partum psychosis that made
the moon rupture, made metaphor, even euphoria,
made one mother want to drown herself in the bath.

She notices she becomes split into the noticer
and the mother here breathing regular
rocking her sleeping boy, and then
the one who'd dreamed she'd hanged from the banister,
remember how baby'd be screaming
and she'd be feebly shushing, feeling her breath constricted,
ears bruised at every shriek—
and she begins weeping for her, that woman she'd been

pitiful in quicksand, beating herself
with bats and hammers, words and scissors
and she's telling her,

> *Look where you'll soon be,*
> *rocking and loving, marvelling*
> *as your little one does*
> *when he wakes, safe, even though he's somewhere*
> *different to where he'd fallen asleep.*

.

Strike

Today of all days
he kicks the ball across the yard
it soars over the wall, smacks
the grandmother in the face—
the boy's force against her cold cheek
her eyes sprout tears, her mouth gasps
and he, eyes fixed at the burning point of contact,
sorries, hands-to-mouth, realises
that sometimes we don't mean
to strike,
but we hurt
and there's nothing we can do
to take it back.

My Son Whittles a Stick for his Father's Birthday

and I'm back: Form 3, the boy who sock-sneaked

his penknife into class, sat at the back in English and Maths,

hand splayed on the desk he'd initialled, stabbing the blade between
each finger,

eyes fixed forward, never at the knife, never missing, never
flinching—

there were bigger things he was stabbing.

Mechanics

Boy has a wire. He bends it when homeworking, listening,
makes shapes of his thinking.
Boy uses it to pick locks, to get into the gubbins of something—
a toy car, an old calculator; the wire does his bidding,
it's the thread of his questions:

> *How does this work? How do I take that apart, figure out*
> *what goes where and what makes what do what?*

The wire is his key, the tool, the instrument of exploring,
a finger inviting him
to not take things as things are given to him.

My daughter's fox on the wall
red as the sky shining on its felt-tip pelt.
The blue eye asking,

Well, will you?
Will you go into the forest
of brightest light?

Bird Prayer III: Red-tailed Hawk, Louisiana

Another morning of it. I sat under the porchway waiting
for the hummingbird on the feeder, but there you were
beyond, in the overgrown corner of the wire fence, there

you perched: a shock, you showing up
in this concrete suburb
and the garden I was afraid to enter.

Were you after the rat skulking our thick grass,
or waiting for lizard-heavy leaves to bend?

I wasn't sure what
to pay attention to, your still
deep gaze or
the way you swooped off—

                  your wing breeze told on next door's pear tree.

Later, a dove flew into our screen-door and we placed it,
dazed, into an old cage. As soon as it came back
to itself with the wild eyes of the newly trapped,
I remembered
and took to the road

and then, the sky.

Leaf River, Mississippi

Where I posed on a rock bare-footed,
floppy hat. You took photographs;
they were anything but black and white.
We walked the abandoned railroad bridge
vulture-high, nothing to hold onto but the sky;
the structure swayed daring us to miss a step—
to press too long on a rotten plank meant
the river would have broken us: you walked
fluent, sure of your gait. I was in terror
of the distant rumble,
the coming thunder of a long-ago train.

Later, you with your gun (in case
of wild boar) shot old cans. I took my naked
self down the riverbank, slid the burnt sienna slip
like I was going back to the clay that made me:
a relief from the heat until the too-fast current
took me and a water moccasin in the same surge
swept us down river faster than my screams came out
but you dived in, caught me—
back in those days when I still wanted to be caught.

Rewilding

Maarmmmaah solid as a boulder
we are bound together—the same rock, rock grown of rock
a crow can rest on us, preen its feathers
dash a nut on our shoulders
it's like this we see across the valley,
the wind blows over the hills
and *Maarmmmaah* hums the old sounds—they send us
to the out of sleep place where we wander with feet
where we tumble on the plateau   where we fly   crow

Still Life

'Something that's called soul, they claim that it never dies and that it lives for ever and seeks for ever and for ever and for evermore.'
- Vincent van Gogh in a letter to his brother Theo, 1880

You crab, poor dab, pulled from the deep,
sea-dregs drained, pincers air-snapped, you on your back.
Did a signal in your DNA say you'd be simmered,
served as supper with lemons and butter?
Did your deadman's finger flick into action—
hope to make a last meal for a glutton?

Instead, sea-creature, rock-dweller
you got a needle to your soft-spot, the brain
and mechanics of movement in slow
shut-down. Posed, you were by a window,
drenched in midday sun, set on a platter
of emerald fabric—an irony not lost
on the last of your thoughts, if
you had any. But those greens—

if it weren't for those greens and all their names
and the brush strokes that set ripples across the canvas,

if it weren't for the sea-voice calling out the turquoise,
stilling your sideways crawl, then the red of you,

the rouged cheek of your shell would have turned
gull-grey, and I would not be here a century on
with your scent tormenting my palate, my ears full
of the pot being hauled-in on a fisherman's song—

and if it weren't for the rapture of colour,
I'd not see the artist lick his brush
or share his hunger.

Captives

I

In the photo: the dungareed monkey thrust
onto her lap; the two, pram-captive
for the Barry Island snapshot. She'd squeezed
the living toy at its neck till it shrieked
and scratched. The child would not release her grasp.

II

Her uncle took her on the skiff, fishing mullet.
She sat on the ice chest, felt their frantic
tails thwacking. When she was asked to reach in for a beer
she caught their gills mouthing—
their milky eyes in terrified
focus meeting hers. She rubbed the slime
across her fringe, shut the lid.

III

As the skirt of the circus bloats
she wants candyfloss, or
a different top — the polo neck,
too close-fitting, makes her spark
when she touches her mother.

The Russian gives her the lion cub.
She asks its name before
they take the photo.   She lets Odessa go
to run mayhem round the hem of the ring.

Free

Even the wire has unfenced, it reaches up
saluting the sun like those stones arranged
to look druidic, but the dog runs honest
bolting over the fairway—all she knows
is space and the scent of the man-made
lake she wants to lap her tongue in, unbridled joy,
she's oblivious to the paralysis of industry
that once hacked this hill, unconscious
of that man's concentration
as he waits, impatient to strike iron:

       doesn't he know that golf balls were once
       made of feathers, that there's a time
       for flight, and a time for watching a creature
       run free, surrendering to the natural will
       we all once followed.

Negative Space

'Is not the harvesting of light the only work that matters?'
Nigel Jenkins

Beyond the redgra, parts of the school
I'd never seen, like down a dip

where there were trees
I hadn't known about.
She made me meet them
with my hands, form impressions

of bark with clay, let a leaf sit in my palm, then
draw from memory of touch. I began to wear
an old man's coat and let my hair loose

after she told me to slacken
my eyes, to see outside my usual
way of seeing. She called it negative space,

Ma, the parts we don't notice. Not the branches,
deep browns and mossy limbs, not
the leaves' spread or the whole tree's crown,

but the shapes in between where the sky shined
through;
                the tree's unconscious—and mine.

Forest Haiku

cock and balls sprayed on an oak—
deep seated desire
to be that enduring

Guide for a Friend

i.m. Heather

I. Waters
Your hair kingfisher blue, you led us upriver to swim
in the pool the other side of the rapids— you kicked off
your clothes and dived in, no hesitation.
I stood on the bank afraid of what might swallow me
if I allowed myself to follow. The walk
back over bridges, through gates
that you held open. Closed behind me.

II. Car
As if you intuited. I was on the driveway neither going
nor coming, sat crying at a locked steering wheel
and you phoned. With all you had going on, I tried
to make my voice sound like it had its bearings,
asked repeatedly about your treatments, your heart,
the kids, poems, but in the slow lane you overtook
those racing questions, had me in tow with your voice so it felt
you were passenger alongside me, navigating as I wept.

III. Examens
Soon after, you sent me a life-line, to still the swarm of bees—
your process of weighing daily feelings, a way of praying into notice:
you shared your heart-talk with failings and woes
and the method to hold space for some sort of god to compose
a response, a perspective working itself out as does a poem.
I'd never read anything that spoke to my heart so directly.
The last entry, your god had written to you and today, you spoke too

> *Still here*
> *you know how to find me*

'You Must Wear Your Eyes Out, as Others Their Knees'

R.S. Thomas

Bring to the making table an axe, chop—
snap shards over a bent knee,
give your hands blisters if you must, but
        leave:

walk your eyes across the field, to the river's under,
go feed a horse, let its muzzle set your palm on fire
lay your hands to the grass
or a deflated ball,
        soak-up colour, shape, shadow
or sit,   witness
the inner/outer
        both are hidden, both translating.

                            Let yourself
be   not making,
not seeking.

If god exists
god's in the splinter.

First Response

After Robert Hayden's 'Those Winter Sundays'

Even the nights when the house was sleeping
my father got up to his alerter shrieking—
sleptwalked into his clothes laid out like a given-up ghost,
then with hands frozen from scraping windshield ice
he entered blazing houses, put other people's fires out.

I'd wake too and stay awake fretting till the car, two streets away,
the lullaby of smoke creeping under my door
and his sigh as he'd sink back to bed and me into sleep—
no more fear about the 'shout' he wouldn't talk about in the morning,

not as if I'd ask or cared what rages he had to calm,
bodies he had to carry, only *Daddy, paint with me!*
What did I know as I walked on his back the next day and scratched
at the embers in his hair, of what it took when tired-out
for him to paint me a butterfly in colours so warm, they still glow.

Keep calm, Mam, and write poetry
let your imagination pull you into a dream

Clairaudience

gives me vertigo when walking, dreamspins
when sleeping, I feel I'm slipping
words merging and upside down-ing
I'm *ben i waered* in my head, *ddim yn siŵr*
if I'm speaking English or Welsh
and when they are mixing, these words are fighting,

not sure if it's poems I'm writing
or some ancestor reactivated
dictating their own trauma, trying
to get attention for what wasn't said
or heard before electric shocks to the system
or the war and trench and malaria, the love lost
the wife-beater, the still born, the yellow fever,
the paint-less painter, the piano-less player.

I'm like that spiritualist in the village hall
with her head dipped, saying
    Shush, I hear you
    but one at a time if I'm to speak for you at all.
One at a time I have to untangle
each voice that makes me unstable,

Dal dy dir my friend says, hold your ground;
I'm learning, it's not hold
while the ground is spinning, it's riding
the soundwaves, holding my nerve
so I hear who and what language is communicating.

ben i waered – topsy turvy   *ddim yn siŵr* – not sure

Last Night My Dream Had Subtitles

I've been bingeing on Scandi dramas,
Welsh language noir series, and because
our daughter has started light-sleeping,
waking at the settling of floorboards
or next door's cat-flap, we sit in whispers,
we have the subtitles on. Last night,
instead of dreaming my dream,
I was reading—the text, and the subtext.

What they Cannot Measure

Evidence suggests
that a stressed mother
will pass harmful hormones
to the foetus. That cortisol
and adrenalin will directly
flow to the unborn child.

These studies entered my blood,
revved up the guilt-organ, sent bile
and lactic acid on the rampage.

Sometimes I wish I'd never pressed charges,
never been believed (finally) so that
days in court would never have happened

and I'd have been at home making a belly
cast, eating pickles, having odd dreams
and defending myself against stretch marks—

but in the house of my bones
when the timbers creak,
they speak of the forest;

I couldn't have been looking forward
to your first words knowing
I'd held mine back.

What She Told Me to Remember When I Was in Court

I am a hummingbird, always on the wing
sweet-seeking,
iridescent in chest, blue-green shines
where my heart beats underneath.

I am a saxophone, slow deep tones,
sultry, street corner player, I make my bones
creak, speak jazz speak.

I am gumbo base, earth taste
spices bubbling on the stove,

below sea-level I am
ships on the Mississippi
floating above me.

I am the band
the whole band playing
do you hear me?

Across the river
across the sky, sea,
do you hear me?

Ceg: Cegin; Mouth: Kitchen

for Elin

Eisteddfod art—the dialect of her walls.
At the room's heart, the table:
hill smell from line-dried linen, a bullion of butter
gleaming on an heirloom dish, ripe fruit and
hothouse tomatoes in a wide-lipped vessel.

She's spaced each offering, arranged plates
to keep our conversation on course, and given
our talk of rivers and language flowing,
the slab of salmon points to the source.

No time for pleasantries; this is urgent.
We pass our words, the bread, the bread-knife;
she teaches me to season slick and slack
parts of my not quite fluent Welsh. I stumble.

It's there on the worktop, the unwrapped gift.
She serves up this delicacy. Tongue—
a meat I've never eaten, its texture
foreign on my own tongue, the warmth of it

hard to swallow. An inherited heaving
works to halt these muscles seeking union, but

nothing is unspoken between us now;
a rush of hunger. Each word shudders on my fork.

Endowment

I
at the mica table, the fire settling,
the rest of the house cold and no-oned. I saw you,
legs too short to touch linoleum
left all night with your paint set
swirling yellows with your brush,
stirring the sunshine into the kitchen, and a dip
of red like a toy you had or didn't have. I saw you pause
before tapping to paper,
the gasp of pleasure as you stepped in
created the whole picture

II
you snatching the bottle from the doorstep
marching to the house of that boy who'd snapped
your dog's snout shut with elastics.
Fire in your eyes, flint in your words,
you flashed your canines through the letterbox
of the boy everyone was afraid of,
snarled as he cowered behind his front door
in a puddle of whimper and piss

III
17, left in Delivery as the nurses in the waiting room
talked strike in whispers. A bit shocked with your new-born,
swirling your finger like a paint brush over her nose, her father's
        thatch of hair,
laying down the hues and shades
for all the beautiful things you hoped she might make.

Healing the Pack

She's leaning, little one, against the beech,
spine to trunk where no one can reach her
hear her pleading, *Tree, swallow me.*

In the fields where there will be houses
her spaniel machine guns the grasses
snouting something in the under
while she's picking her thumb wart
aware of her own scenting, sweat
on the down of her sealed lip
willing an ignoring of itch from poly-cardi,
her scab from the street party—
crust splitting every time she is on bended knee.

I know I'll find her there against that tree
eyes attached to the parting grasses.
I tell her with the only voice she will hear, *Sit;*
I turn her back to the wilds
so she faces the hill below with the housing estate
and the terrible house. I sit her on tree root
remember the cheap daps and Lady Di cut—
I draw her in, let her latch on, be leech to me,
I make it hurt a little, the acknowledgment of arms

and then I am wolf pelt. I wrap hot hood,
animal stink fresh from kill around her until
she slips on the whole hide from ear to claw,

Run, I say,
Run! Hunt down the poet you'll become
bite out her tongue,
teach her what it is to howl.

Bird Prayer IV: Boncath

Welsh for buzzard, I learned, as *I* was carrying
my girl. One pinned her cries to the sky
above our house when I pegged washing,
or sat on a deckchair practising birth-breathing.

Contracting in the bedroom, no panic set in;
I rolled my pregnant self in increasing
circles, mandala-making, remembering
the patterns I'd seen her show in flight.
And at the hour of the new lungs' puling
the roof of our house split with buzzard call.

I've not heard her. I've not seen her since—
except when my little girl sings, or, like now
she's jumping on the trampoline as snow falls

and there's a moment in the gap between
going up and coming down . . .

                    there,

                              in that gap she soars.

NOTES

'She Wouldn't Be Able to Come to You So Often if She Were Alive' from 'Name, Day Forty-Two' a poem by Kim Hyesoon, translated by Don Mee Choi.

'Measuring the Distance' created in response to a lecture by Jon Gower on Raymond Williams' Border Country (for Peak Cymru's Defining the Borders project).

'. . .' inspired by Jonathan Edwards poem, 'Gregory Peck and Sophia Loren'. The line 'That's how my father tells it' comes from his poem.

'Swyn-gân / Summoning' commissioned for the Plethu/Weave project, a collaboration with Literature Wales and National Dance Company Wales to explore how dance and poetry might express aspects of Cynghanedd.

'Orientation' refers to the early 19th century Welsh language poet William Thomas whose Bardic name was Islwyn.

'How the Light Gets In' was an art exhibition and series of public events exploring the mind, mental illness and psychiatric genetics. Funded by the Medical Research Council and curated by Dr Julia M. Thomas and Dr Jamie Lewis. The poem refers to Joan Malloy's 'Unravelling Eve,' a film about post-partum psychosis: https://joanmolloy. com/films

'Rewilding' inspired by the model of a Neanderthal woman and child, constructed by Adrie and Alfons Kennis.

'Still Life' inspired by seeing Vincent van Gogh's oil painting 'A Crab on its Back'. A painting in which van Gogh was exploring Eugène Delacroix' laws of colour.

'Negative Space' refers to *Ma*, a Japanese aesthetic concept meaning blankness, the silence between words, objects, space and the consciousness of space, a void full of possibility.

'You Must Wear Your Eyes Out, as Others Their Knees' from R.S. Thomas' poem, 'Sea-watching'.

'First Response' inspired by Robert Hayden's 'Those Winter Sundays' which pays tribute to his father's devotion to him. The 'shout' in my poem refers to the alerter calls my father, a fire-fighter, would receive all throughout the night.

'Ceg: Cegin; Mouth: Kitchen' National Poet of Wales Ifor ap Glyn coined the phrase: 'Gwell Cymraeg slac neu Saesneg slic' (better slack Welsh than slick English), a mantra for Welsh learners.

PUBLICATIONS

The author wishes to acknowledge the following publications/ platforms for publishing versions of poems in this collection:

Atlanta Review; Arachne Press; The Lampeter Review; Writing Motherhood, Seren Press; Poetry Wales; The Pikeville Review; Wales Arts Review; Iceflo Press; The Crunch; Plethu Project: Literature Wales and National Dance Company Wales; Zoomorphic Magazine; Manchester Metropolitan University; Hiraeth Erzolirzoli: A Wales - Cameroon Anthology, Hafan Books; Tis the Season to be Mindful, Collective Creative Voices Minded, Blurb Books; The Outposted Project; #MeToo: Rallying Against Sexual Assault and Harassment, Fair Acre Press; Peak Cymru, Defining the Borders.

ACKNOWLEDGEMENTS

Thank you to everyone who supported me on this long journey to finally finish this book and help me find the courage to release the work. There are many people to thank. I begin with my family, several long lines of hardworking, working class, storytellers. In particular my nan, Clara, who sat me by the fire to learn to listen and record; my Uncle Cyril who gave me my first poetry book (smelling of the miners' library); my Uncle Clarry for feathers and my first thesaurus and Aunty Pat for fruit salads as I worked in their house overlooking the field with the buzzard. My aunties and cousins who shared stories, particularly Aunty Vano, Aunty Gloria and Aunty Norah. I thank grandparents who I never met in person, but continue to show up and show me something of myself.

I have been fortunate to have had many inspiring teachers, especially Mr Clifford James who taught me to love poetry as a physical presence and to feel it fully. Richard Gwyn, Ifor ap Glyn, Angela Ball, John Freeman and Shelagh Weeks. I'm grateful for Jill Teague my cherished poetry therapy mentor and all my peer support group at the International Academy for Poetry Therapy. To every student I have ever taught, you taught me much more.

To Cerith and Eiddwen for letting me stay in the forge to write. Poet Robert Walton, thank you for encouraging me to share my work. To friends who have supported the poet writing: MacNair Randall (for helping me believe. You are my heart's treasure), Julia Thomas (for truth and 'making art'), Dylan Jones Wood (am sgyrsiau dwfn). Thank you to Jan Villarubia and Lynn Avant for your poems and support of mine. Emma Howells-Davies (thanks for keeping me on task). Kate Allday and Cath Stephens thank you for a long creative friendship.

I am grateful to my writing group, Inklings: Katherine Stansfield, Mark Blayney, Emily Blewitt Susie Wildsmith, Hillary Watson, Kate North, Chrsitina Thatcher, Zillah Bowes, Rhian Edwards.

Thanks also to my Hay Festival Writers at Work friends, especially Louise Walsh, Catrin Clarke, Rebecca Parfitt (also an Inkling) and Ben Wildsmith. My work has also been supported in poetry residencies by: The Landmark Trust, The Wales Arts Review, Moravian Academy Pennsylvania (thanks to the Puleo family). I am grateful to Louise Richards at Literature Wales for connecting me to deeply inspiring community poetry projects. To my friend, poet Heather Trickey (you are deeply missed). My friends who sent me podcasts and took me on walks: Emma Shepherd and Bethan Reynolds; to childhood friends Pritch, Cerys, Andrea and Stish who always support my work. Thanks, Will Lawton for letting me speak some poems on your wonderful lockdown album Salt of the Earth (it got me back to myself), to Stacey Blythe for creative petrol, to Jon Dafydd-Kidd for much needed mentoring. Nik and Pam for cakes and thoughtfulness. Thanks, El Davis for support and creative processing. Thank you, Claire Akers-Dyer, for reminding me to return to joy. Mark Boulton-Brown always believing in me, and Patrick Jones and Jon Gower for years of solidarity. Tom for looking after the children at a moment's notice. Mab Jones for getting me over the last hurdle, and Terry Lewis producer of our many poetry radio programmes. I am forever grateful to Graham and Grant at New Pathways. Rhian Elizabeth, where would I be without you? Lost.

Thank you to my local ancient woodland, Coed Dyffryn Dowlais, to Nant Ty Crwyn, and the ash tree for my continued renewal and belonging. And to Nicholas Twilley, shaman, whose course The Art in Listening was instrumental in my poetic process.

Thank you to Zoë Brigley who through a Society of Authors grant mentored me through the final stages to better organise this collection into a shape that made sense, teaching me how poems can speak to one another. I was moved by your insights and care, Zoë.

To E. Good, a librarian. Thanks to your suitcase for holding and carrying my poems.

To my publisher Stuart Bartholomew, thank you for valuing my writing and for your sensitivity and care of me in the process of releasing this collection to the world. I am thrilled to join the Verve Poetry pack! I'm grateful to artist, Lucy Campbell for the use of her beautiful image Axis Mundi for the cover of this book.

To my beloved friend and Guide, Chris Torrance. We're at the humming pole, aren't we?

To Mam and Dad. Artists. I love you and admire you both. You gave me all the tools, and paid attention, showed me wonder and beauty, taught me to love who I am and what I come from. And to all the dogs of our pack, thank you for heightening my senses.

Thank you, Michael, you keep reminding me to look after the poet and the poetry, to get out into the woods, to be inspired, to see where the light falls, especially on our beautiful children.

For Gwynnie and Gwennie. Thank you, my lovelies, for sharing the way you see (and say) the world in all its truth and wonder and for letting me share it. For keeping your mam believing that poetry is a powerful force that connects us. It always will.

The author would like to acknowledge the award of a Literature Wales Writer's Bursary supported by the Arts Council of Wales, for the purpose of developing this collection. And also, an Authors' Foundation grant from the Society of Authors.

Eighty Four:

Poems on Male Suicide, Vulnerability, Grief and Hope

With an introduction from editor Helen Calcutt

Eighty Four was originally a new anthology of poetry on the subject of male suicide in aid of CALM. Poems were donated to the collection by Andrew McMillan, Salena Godden, Anthony Anaxogorou, Katrina Naomi, Ian Patterson, Caroline Smith, Carrie Etter, Peter Raynard, Joelle Taylor, while a submissions window yielded many excellent poems on the subject from hitherto unknown poets we are thrilled to have been made aware of.

We hope this book will shed light on an issue that is cast in shadow, and which is often shrouded in secrecy and denial. If we don't talk, we don't heal and we don't change. In Eighty Four we are all talking. Are you listening?

Available in paperback:
ISBN: 978 1 912565 13 9
188 pages • 216 x 138 • 56 poems
£11.99

And on eBook:
ISBN: 978 1 912565 79 5
£6.99

Where Else:

An International Hong Kong Poetry Anthology

With an introduction from the editors Jennifer Wong, Jason Eng Hun Lee & Tim Tim Cheng

Featuring both established and emerging Hong Kong poets across generations and continents, this unique anthology offers a glimpse into an exciting, diverse range of voices that make up the diasporic imagination of the contemporary Hong Kong poetry community. Adopting a diasporic approach, the anthology encompasses both native Hong Kong writers as well as expatriate and mixed-race voices who were born or have lived in the city.

'We are Hong Kongers to the core and will defend our cantankerous vivid imagination against all invaders and occupiers. Our poetry is the ultimate expression of freedom and is a harbinger of all that is wondrous!' - Marilyn Chin

Available in paperback:
ISBN: 978 1 913917 36 4
252 pages • 216 x 138 • 106 poems
£14.99

And on eBook:
ISBN: 978 1 913917 79 1
£9.99

ABOUT VERVE POETRY PRESS

Verve Poetry Press is a prize-winning press that focused initially on meeting a local need in Birmingham - a need for the vibrant poetry scene here in Brum to find a way to present itself to the poetry world via publication. Co-founded by Stuart Bartholomew and Amerah Saleh, it now publishes poets from all corners of the UK - poets that speak to the city's varied and energetic qualities and will contribute to its many poetic stories.

Added to this is a colourful pamphlet series, many featuring poets who have performed at our sister festival - and a poetry show series which captures the magic of longer poetry performance pieces by festival alumni such as Polarbear, Matt Abbott and Imogen Stirling.

The press has been voted Most Innovative Publisher at the Saboteur Awards, and has won the Publisher's Award for Poetry Pamphlets at the Michael Marks Awards.

Like the festival, we strive to think about poetry in inclusive ways and embrace the multiplicity of approaches towards this glorious art.

www.vervepoetrypress.com
@VervePoetryPres
mail@vervepoetrypress.com